The Longevity is Killing Us Series – Book Two

YOU PLEDGE

WHAT?

Richard W. Farwell

RUGGED MAN PUBLISHING

You Pledge What?

The Longevity is Killing Us Series – Book Two

Printed in the United States of America.

Cover design by Lyndsey Barrett, www.AreteDesignStudio.com.

ISBN-10: 0985314923
ISBN-13: 978-0-9853149-2-7

Published by Rugged Man Publishing.
www.ruggedmanpublishing.com.

Dedicated to all the world's children
whose future is being mortgaged by their parents

Table of Contents

Forward... Maybe!

Just in case you have not recently seen in writing what most of us Americans have memorized, here is our Pledge of Allegiance to the American Flag:

"I pledge allegiance to the flag of the United States of America and to the Republic for which it stands; one nation under God, indivisible, with liberty and justice for all."

As the following chapters will detail, there have been a few monumental changes to the principles of this pledge based upon Webster's Dictionary. Since these changes have been developing over many decades, it may take an election or two to get us back to the basic principles of our country... or redefine them.

Each of us citizens must soon decide if we still are a Republic, one nation under God, happy with our divisiveness and serious about liberty and justice for all.

Regardless of your political lean, some facts cannot be ignored in spite of cause or blame. Their implications profoundly affect nearly all of us... some more than others. Here are a few of our biggies:

- Poverty levels are the highest since the 1960s.
- Between 2007 and 2010, average family wealth dropped 39%. While the real estate market is near its bottom, stock market gains have only helped a few as volume is down.

- While more nurses are being hired, teachers and policemen are being laid off with substantial, but unfunded, benefits.
- Combat vets are returning home to few jobs but plenty of suicides.
- Teen joblessness is near all-time highs as our unemployment/underemployment rates remain high.
- Student debt loads are difficult to cover in a poor job market, regardless of or if credentials earned.
- Budget deficits and debt continue to rise, adding to a shrinking work force's obligations.
- Nearly half of American households have one or more members dependent upon government.
- Unfunded entitlement obligations are estimated at $100 trillion and growing as we age.
- Our high and rising health care costs are the highest as a percentage of economic growth and per capita in the world!
- "Obesebetes" says it all.
- Cities are going bankrupt. States like California are too, but won't admit it.
- Looming budget cuts and tax increases (fiscal cliff)

will receive more temporary fixes by year end. What military will defend the free world if we cannot? Do we need to spend more each year on our military than the next 17 largest militaries worldwide... combined?

- Economic growth is slow and restricted by high costs of dependency and fairness policies directed at greed. Not since the 1930s has a recovery from a recession been this weak.

Thanks to Silicon Valley, high tech allows business to cut costs and make a profit while keeping employment down, often through outsourcing. At least they create plenty of applications for smartphones, so users can be distracted from the above and avoid critical thinking about a scary tomorrow.

I hope that as you travel through each of the following pledge issues, you will conclude, as have I that happiness, success, prosperity, opportunity and our position as leader of the free world are at risk and time is short for fixing.

... and to the ~~Republic~~ Elected for which it stands...

As defined in our dictionary, a Republic means "the supreme power rests with the electorate."

For numerous reason, we the Shallow Electorate, have opted to transfer our supreme power to the Elected while allowing campaign $/Super-PACs and the media on both sides of the aisle to manipulate our thoughts and actions.

A small sign that we may have an awakening was the 2010 elections when a new House of Representatives supported the Tea Party movement, which drew a line in the sand (I call jelly – JLE – just like Europe). The result was lack of compromise. The baton was then thrown to our central banker (the Federal Reserve/Fed) to stimulate the economy. They have bought bonds and driven down interest rates to historic lows... to no avail other than creating a bond bubble.

Does that remind you at all of the real estate bubble the Fed created in the early 2000s followed by our Elected pushing financial institutions to lend money to home buyers who couldn't afford the payments? We elected them, then reelected them and then bought, through our investments, the packaged mortgages that created the Great Recession of 2008. Stop blaming Wall Street. Check the mirror... we are a Republic!

Why do we allow a tax code that means 46% of Americans paid no federal income tax in 2011? Sure, many of them paid Social Security taxes last year but our Elected spent that too and replaced it with a promissory note unlikely to be fully paid without more debt.

Just this last July, a federally appointed state budget crisis task force co-chaired by Paul Volcker, former Fed chairman, and Richard Ravitch, past Lieutenant Governor of New York, made an alarming report.

Major threats to states' fiscal health were identified: Medicaid spending, underfunded retirement promises, budgetary gimmicks and volatile tax revenues.

Those who bear risk limit risk. If bankers, other corporate executives, stockholders and elected officials bore risks, they would limit risks. But no! We, the Shallow Electorate, must bear the risk of bailouts (i.e., too big to fail, etc.). Why? Because we have transferred our supreme power and then opened our wallets and forced future generations to cover debt and promises.

Does it seem to you that our votes are not working? Perhaps too much power to the Elected (statism) is not just hurting our economy, but our moral and spiritual values as well.

Perhaps we all need to do some critical thinking like Congressman Rush Holt, Democrat from New Jersey. As the only physicist in Congress, he suggests we all should try thinking like a scientist. We should not just ask how something works or what it means, but seek empirical evidence we can explain to others. It can be used daily when purchasing goods or especially when seeking a career path.

Speaking of empirical evidence, how about this:

"The significant problems we face cannot be solved at the same level of thinking as we were at when we created them." Albert Einstein

"Again, you cannot connect the dots looking forward; you can only connect them looking backward. So you have to trust that the dots will somehow connect in your future. You have to trust in something – your gut, destiny, life, karma, whatever. This approach has never let me down, and it has made all the difference in my life." Steve Jobs

In 1787, Ben Franklin was asked what sort of government our new nation would have. His answer: "A Republic, if you can keep it."

The question we must now ask is... can we get it back?

... one nation, under ~~God~~ human nature

There is no question America has changed in the last 236 years... and primarily for the better. We are still the most powerful nation on earth, and 85% of Americans still believe in Heaven.

That said, the changes that have been developing in recent decades to address numerous challenges have resulted in a gradual and soon to be overwhelming mortgage on the future. The changes include economic, political, social and moral.

The bottom line and not so obvious cause is that America has drifted away from our original religious principles allowing human nature to dominate.

Before I share with you a heavenly choice and then some hell on earth issues, a recent quote from columnist Thomas Friedman should clarify the difference between thinking once (that's human nature) and thinking twice (critical analysis). Imagine you are on a job interview. This is what the interviewer may be thinking. "Can this person add value every hour, every day – more than a worker in India, a robot or a computer?"

Welcome to the real world of high tech globalization and its revolution. There is no way human nature can prepare one for such an interview or future. It's much easier to rely upon high tech smartphone applications for distractions while munching on a burger with fries.

Instant gratification is the primary goal of human nature... not work ethic, sacrifice, serving the poor, sick, enslaved, and oppressed. Granted, some Americans (young and old) suffer from overweight through no fault of their own. Most, however, experience "obesebetes" by allowing human nature to control.

A great article appeared in the 4/16/12 issue of Time magazine entitled "Rethinking the Hereafter – Heaven Can't Wait."

The contrasting views of Heaven were fascinating. Some endure a sinful, fallen world in search of a reward of eternal rest... which includes passing through the pearly gates.

Others seek bodily resurrection in which God brings together the heaven and the earth in a wholly new, wholly redeemed creation. A quote from one of the article's contributors clarifies this position. "Heaven isn't just a place you go... it's how you live your life." J. Blanchard

Both concepts of Heaven can motivate, be it a heavenly afterlife with a place reserved for the believer or actually changing one's priorities here and now, i.e., the environment, soul saving and acts of selflessness and love.

I also enjoyed the article's inclusion of Heaven based upon religions including Buddhism, Hinduism, Islam, Judaism, Mormonism and Taoism.

Be it bliss or work, deeds, action, what I see happening in America is different. I see many, even those 85% who believe in Heaven, act as though they don't while attempting to live as long and costly and painful a life as possible.

"Just as courage imperils life, fear protects it." Leonardo da Vinci (my guess is that he captured the first part of his line from a hero and the last three words from human nature).

The primary result of this fear of death, this placing human nature first in line, combined with our demographics, is high and rising healthcare costs. They are a major contributor to our $ trillions in unfunded entitlement liabilities, budget deficits and rising debt.

A doctor's Hippocratic Oath is respected and extra test procedures and hospital stays are a result of being compensated based upon units delivered and attempting to avoid malpractice lawsuits. Can you believe that one-third of all healthcare costs is paperwork!

Welcome to the most costly form of human nature... and be assured that no politician will challenge seniors and the seriously ill with these truths.

"I fear that Congress's decisions would be dictated by noise, not sense; by meanness, not greatness; by ignorance, not learning; by contracted hearts, not large souls." John Adams, 1776

"We must move forward with malice toward none, with charity for all, with firmness in the right, as God gives us to see the right." Abe Lincoln

"Humanly speaking, it is impossible. But with God everything is possible." Jesus Christ

Sorry, but it sure looks like America is going to wait for God's wrath as an awakening.

... ~~indivisible~~ totally divided...

Before the 1960s, America was one economy with both of our major political parties connected to private enterprise. As the public sector union movement expanded and the private sector started to disassociate itself from private unions, our one economy then became two.

As Daniel Henninger wrote in the Wall Street Journal this last July, Lyndon Johnson passed the building blocks of The Great Society, notably Medicare, Medicaid and the Voting Rights Act of 1965. Henninger described these events as moral efficacy... public spending was now a public good by producing desired effects.

David Brooks, another columnist, argues that in recent decades, and regardless of party affiliation, with a few exceptions, Presidents and Congress have "layered on regulations and loopholes, creating a form of state capitalism in which big business thrives because they have political connections and small businesses struggle."

There are numerous other economic issues that divide us:

LEFT	RIGHT
Pension/healthcare funding	We cannot afford it
Discretion to change or adopt complex rules based upon fairness; intervention more important than certainty	Rules based (rules of law) and predictable fiscal/monetary policies
More stimulus and debt	Austerity/budget cuts

LEFT	RIGHT
Force business to bring capital and jobs back to USA	First bring predictability/certainty
Improve infrastructure	Yes, when we can afford it
Limit crony capitalism	Limit state capitalism
Increase tax rate to increase tax revenue	Reduce tax rates and reform code to increase tax revenue

"Structural change will only succeed if accompanied by a moral argument." Arthur C. Brooks

Exactly! That is what changed in the 1960s for the Democrats. Even our founders emphasized our unalienable right to pursue happiness, not possession of property. Here are some of the moral issues of today:

LEFT	RIGHT
Security	Risk
Comfort	Effort
Stability	Innovation
Income redistribution tax	Earned success
Cooperate/negotiate	On the wrong road
Social justice	Government should not decide
Fairness	Freedom
More government	Less government

LEFT	RIGHT
Hope and change	Personal sacrifice and responsibility
Maintain complex tax, legal, entitlement, education policies	Reform them all; do not steal from our children
Blame and criticism	Jobs and our future

Considering that two-thirds of our federal budget is entitlements and interest on our debt, neither party can succeed without serious budget cuts, and we must pay bond interest. Do we reform the welfare model or rebalance it?

Even Warren Buffett, a left-leaning wealthy capitalist warns "the costs of public sector retirees is a time bomb!" Why? When governors and mayors can't afford salary increases demanded by public unions, they offer big pension increases. That bill comes due after they are out of office, and we are out of money.

In 1976, the margin of victory in the presidential election was an average of 10 percentage points. In 27 states, the margin was less than 7 percent!

In 2008, the margin of victory in the presidential election was an average of 17 percentage points with blowouts in 29 states! In only 7 states was the winning percentage points less than 5!

Now, voter polarization is greater than ever... red more red and blue more blue. Only a handful of swing states will decide the presidency and control of Congress.

Our country is more divided than ever before... politically, economically and morally. Both parties have strong supporters. The differences are clear.

The question is... not which party will win, but will the winner be a fixer?

... with liberty and justice for ~~all~~ some.

Liberty is defined as "freedom to choose and freedom from arbitrary control, compulsion and constraint."

Justice is defined as "the power to uphold what is just, lawful and right; impartiality and fairness" (treat all sides alike regardless of feelings, interests or inclinations against any side).

If liberty is freedom to choose without arbitrary control and justice is fairness to uphold what is lawful, then laws passed based upon fairness should really be fair. Fair means treat all sides alike, not make them alike. Fair is freedom from prejudice for or against any side.

Once laws are in place (i.e., Dodd/Frank, Obamacare, etc.) and especially if it takes years to define them, then liberty is attacked and freedom from arbitrary control and constraint is lost.

We are allowing, through our handing over supreme power to the Elected, a poor definition of fairness resulting in laws (so called justice) that unfairly take away our liberty resulting in divisiveness.

When poorly defined justice takes away liberty and God's wrath is withheld, complexity and divisiveness, in the name of questionable fairness, means shallowness supports upward mobility of our supreme power. The result is a more costly government. If not restrained, then state capitalism (socialism) dominates society.

As economic growth weakens, even Keynesians agree that more debt stimulus must ultimately be replaced with private industry/capitalism. I also agree that austerity is best exercised in a boom, not in weakness. Even Mr. Keynes understood about selling high, not low.

The longer the delay and greater the debt, the risk of chronic unemployment trending to structural unemployment rises. As work skills weaken and high-tech globalization rockets forward, a permanent underclass of young, dependent citizens will be unable to cover existing and ever-expanding obligations of an aging society.

Oh, and where does that leave our combat veterans returning home with such poor job prospects?

Capitalism, with all of its faults, still generates lots of jobs and tax revenues to cover the cost of its greed, excesses, the truly needy and even reduces our debts.

At some point in the near future, our Shallow Electorate, especially the young and their elders (that covers just about all of us) must acknowledge that capitalism is incentives to take risk, resulting in success or failure. Rejecting it in favor of debt and dependency is a grave mistake that undermines liberty and the true principle of fairness. (I purposely use the word grave for emphasis!)

Justice is so fair in our country that we now have a severely complex and costly legal system where the penalty must precisely fit the crime, + or – a bunch of ******s.

This leaves our Elected, often understandably but foolishly, with the obligation to set new regulations to control behavior, which burdens business in the name of fairness.

Those who are smart, have money, or both, can work these complex laws (and tax code as well) and seldom get caught.

If caught, they will happily pay the small fine.

Until we severely punish all serious crimes forcing a think-twice attitude, we will all suffer... in the name of justice and fairness. Sound like liberty and freedom to you?

"And can the liberties of a nation be thought secure when we have removed their only firm basis, a conviction in the minds of the people that these liberties are of the gift of God? That they are not to be violated but with His wrath? Indeed I tremble for my country when I reflect that God is just; that His justice cannot sleep forever." Thomas Jefferson

Mr. Jefferson, I cannot agree with you more. I think He is awakened, and I tremble as well.

Conclusion... in more ways than one

Do you really believe that legislative bodies or central bankers will solve economic problems in aging societies like we have today? They will not, neither through more debt nor austerity.

Only pro-business regulations including major reforms to entitlements, taxes and legal policies will fix what is ailing the U.S. and many other countries as well. How can that happen if politicians think they will lose votes? Better to just give waivers like our Health and Human Services agency is now doing to buy a few votes while undermining some great welfare reform signed into law in 1996 by President Clinton.

Perhaps fine tuning around the edges and moving the political argument away from economic growth toward moral issues is the new election norm... or has it been with us for a while?

Did you notice how even the chairman of our central bank just recently added happiness as a mandate to join low inflation and high employment?

Even the Bank of International Settlements (BIS), the organization that represents the world's central banks, has concluded that recent global easing and stimulus has not helped much while taking pressure off of governments to reform. The imbalances throughout the developed world are now affecting emerging economies as well. To quote the BIS in its latest annual report, "The question is not whether governments must adjust, but how?"

"The result is that year after year, we slip further down the redistribution road, dissatisfied with the growing welfare state, but with no morally satisfying arguments to make a change that entails any personal sacrifice." Arthur C. Brooks

Looking back to see forward, per Mr. Steven Jobs and countless other great minds with designations galore, one fact trumps all others. The past does not reveal any time in history where a large developed country with an aging and dependent society faced with a high-tech, highly competitive global environment succeeded economically by using anti-growth, pro-dependency policies. Therefore, old strategies do not work even though "all the ways of a man are right in his own eyes." Proverbs 16:25

Germany, for example, is an aging and highly regulated social capitalist economy with a very skilled work force. One major difference: It is not being overwhelmed by entitlements even though there is a strong union/business connection. If there is one big difference between Germany and the U.S., it is that our per capita healthcare cost is double theirs.

Yes, we have been given clues about the future by visionaries, but even those don't seem to be helping this world. For example, how do you react to today's headlines after reading this quote from Confucius, "If a man takes no thought about what is distant, he will find sorrow near at hand."? I see very little evidence of critical thinking by our Elected or Electorate... do you? Very little doesn't mean none. Twenty-five hundred years later, someone was listening to the great Chinese philosopher. A freshman congressman from Wisconsin joined a handful of others to reduce taxpayer risk at Fannie Mae and Freddie Mac. No one listened. He tried again in 2002, also to no avail. Paul Ryan did give thought about what is distant, and now the sorrow from the 2008 Great Recession still surrounds us. It seems that the blame game trumps critical thinking in today's world. While both of our major political parties share some of the responsibility, the blame rests with us. What a shame!

Today, we have a predictable crisis, and while waiting is worse, there seems to be only old strategies fine-tuned... and they will not work... and that also goes for temporary central banker actions of late. Sorry, but we are beyond the point of our elected/appointed leaders solving anything monumental... and this is a big one indeed. Look no further than Europe and Japan if you want further proof.

Yes, President Obama, there is hope if we are willing to change. The change I refer to is for the Electorate (that's us voters in a Republic) to hold human nature at bay while we commit to the only solution with a chance of success.

While we all should attempt to have a long, healthy life, it is the short, unhealthy one at the end that is the key. When ill health puts us seniors and other seriously disabled Americans in a mental/physical crisis allowing human nature to favor debt over dirt, it has dishonored our heroes and has undermined the future of America and our children.

This is the election, the only election, that can bring us back to leadership of the free world. More importantly, it is an election that re-ignites the human spirit that has made us great since our birth. It is one's election of self-inflicted austerity no politician would ever suggest. It places one's deity, loved ones and society ahead of selfish, human nature-driven dependency.

Be assured that if you do restrict costly end-of-life care by clearly defining those wishes in a living will/medical directive, your loved ones will appreciate your sacrifice for their benefit. Imagine the powerful voting block that would develop when children, parents and grandparents join together in preventative care and selfless acts. No politician would dare spend the savings without authority from the supreme power (we are the owners).[1]

Since we still live in a free country that is rapidly changing, the choice is ours. We did build our family, and only we can assure its success as this unique scenario develops. Of course, we also can just shrug, with human nature at our side, and force all to await malaise, economic disaster or worse. It is disrespectful for citizens to place their own selfish dependency above their country and its heroes. When those citizens are parents and grandparents, the negative impact upon their offspring's future is ignorant and unforgivable.

If such an attitude and the relinquishing of power is the continuing choice of our Electorate, consider reelecting our current President with a divided House and Senate. It will at least accelerate our pending calamity, and awakening that would be delayed but not avoided under Romney/Ryan (Look no further than Mr. Ryan's Medicare reform. It does not apply to seniors 55 and over. We cannot wait that long!). Regardless of who wins on 11/6/12, there will be

---

1 For reference, please see my book, "Longevity is Killing Us," on amazon.com.

aggressive protests by the losers.

These unique times could very well be the first time in our history that the supreme power of the Electorate can save our Republic, place one's God above human nature, become indivisible again and bring back liberty and justice for all.

Imagine if our supreme effort to reduce deficits, debt and dependency was multiplied by Europe and Japan (both also aging and developed societies). The result would be improved economic growth and budget surpluses. Debt as a percentage of growth would drop. Funds would be available to rebuild infrastructure and education systems. And yes, there would also be enough left over to help the truly needy and the globe's environment.

It all must start here... and now... with us seniors.

About the Author

Rick Farwell is married with two children and nine grandchildren. He is financially secure, having no pension other than Social Security. He and his wife, Darlene, worked hard, lived conservatively, and saved regularly to now enjoy a comfortable retirement (thank you 401(k)!).

In his early twenties after college, Rick enlisted in the U.S. Navy, serving as a radar operator on a Grumman S2-A (anti-submarine aircraft). He was a sailor but never on a ship. It was thrilling to have the squadron commander as his pilot!

During his nearly fifty-year career in the financial services industry, he attained the level of head office manager in the Savings and Loan industry, worked his way up to CEO of a nationally renowned credit union, and eventually owned his own financial planning business advising clients in maintaining and increasing their wealth through two tumultuous decades.

Before retiring, Rick was a Certified Financial Planner, a Certified Fund Specialist, a Certified Retirement Counselor, a licensed insurance agent and a stockbroker.

His passion grows daily as he attempts to help the world understand that the answer to solving current economic challenges lies not with government but with individuals currently unwilling to make the tough choices for the welfare of their children and grandchildren.

You can follow Rick on his blog: www.rickfarwell.com.

Made in the USA
Monee, IL
04 November 2026

67352880R00020